This Time This Place

This Time This Place

Susan Suntree

SHANTI ARTS PUBLISHING
BRUNSWICK, MAINE

This Time This Place

Published by Shanti Arts Publishing

Designed by Shanti Arts Designs

Cover image by Dolores Carlos and used with her permission

Shanti Arts LLC
193 Hillside Road
Brunswick, Maine 04011
shantiarts.com

Printed in the United States of America

ISBN: 978-1-962082-94-5 (softcover)

Library of Congress Control Number: 2026931619

This collection is dedicated
to poet and mentor Gary Snyder.

CONTENTS

IMAGES

All images appearing in this book are in the public domain and available on Wikimedia Commons.

[14] Pierre-Antoine Poiteau and Alexandre-Pierre-François Robert-Dumesnil, *Delphinium ajacis* (rocket larkspur), 1828. *Flore générale de France de Loiseleur-Deslongchamps.*

[18] Edward Step, *Polygonum fagopyrum* (buckwheat), 1895. *Wayside and Woodland Blossoms: A Pocket Guide to British Wild-flowers for the Country Rambler.*

[24] James Sowerby, John Boswell, et al, *Symphytum officinale* (common comfrey), 1863. *English Botany, or, Coloured Figures of British Plants.*

[28] Benedetto Bordiga, *Platanus occidentalis* (American sycamore), 1794. *Storia delle piante forastiere le più importanti nell'uso medico, od economico.*

[33] Sydenham Edwards and John Lindley, *Iris tenax* (toughleaf iris), 1820s. *Edwards' Botanical Register, or, Ornamental Flower-garden and Shrubbery.*

[35] James Sowerby and William Curtis, *Crepis barbata* (slender hawksbeard), 1787. *Curtis's Botanical Magazine,* Volume 1.

[36] Sydenham Edwards and John Lindley, *Lupinus sabinianus* (Sabin's lupine), 1820s. *Edwards' Botanical Register, or, Ornamental Flower-garden and Shrubbery.*

[39] Mary Elizabeth Parsons, *Nemophila insignis* (baby-blue eyes), 1902. *The Wild Flowers of California; Their Names, Haunts, and Habits.*

[44] Sydenham Edwards and John Lindley, *Eschscholzia californica* (California poppy), 1820s. *Edwards' Botanical Register, or, Ornamental Flower-garden and Shrubbery.*

ACKNOWLEDGMENTS

The songs of many ancestors infuse poetry's on-going work. Along with the Old Teachers, I am deeply grateful for the comradery of Tom Laiches, Julia Conner, Chris Ferris, and Zoey Zimmerman, with whom I write weekly. Thanks to 18th Street Art Center where I maintained a studio while composing this book. I am deeply grateful for the many people who, for years, have offered me their on-going support. I am steadied by the love of my family: my daughter, Califia Suntree, and her husband Sam Rozell; my sisters, Peggy Watson and Ginger Stout; my brother and his wife, Ted and Melinda Stout. In this uneasy era, I feel keenly the love and support of so many friends, near and far. Thank you, dear ones! We go forward together. It has been a creative pleasure to publish this book under the guidance of Shanti Arts Press editor, Christine Cote. Poet and haiku teacher Richard Modiano's excellent instruction enhanced my appreciation of this venerable form, and several of the poems were inspired by the garden at Beyond Baroque Literary Center in Venice, California, where I was Richard's student. Gratefully, poet Gary Snyder long ago introduced me to Asian poetry and poetic forms. David Hinton translated the Chinese Tang Dynasty (8th century) poet Tu Fu's poem "Spring Landscape." Tu Fu experienced the deprivations and upheaval of war even as he kept his poems secured against his heart while seeking safety for himself and his family.

"The country in ruins, rivers and mountains continue.
The city grows lush with spring."

—Tu Fu

Delphinium ajacis

CALIFORNIA COAST

—Anders Gustave Aldrin "California Coast"

Three red roofs on a sea-roar cliff
      three boxes—clapboard, glass,
azure houses set at the verge
                of a slow flowing continent.
A luxuriant blue-green rolls into trenches
        foaming crests carried
                  all the way from China
    pounding rocks and iron red dirt
foundation and yard once layered
                beneath an older ocean
a sea floor burst through cracks and volcano mouths
                from the earth's deep-down fluid well.
And beneath: the earth's own fire
And before:
      stars
         stars
           stars

RAGS

Shadows stacked in the rag basket
        too many holes to sop up spills
   shabby flags
      once waved over miseries and sad decisions.
Shred those old clothes--
      insulation for another bare cold attic.
Welcome to the sea-blue shelf above the washer
   a fresh batch
      faultless, clean, folded.

River

willow pliant water flow
                    unfurls into estuary
                                     the sea's delight
                            welcoming
                    hungering
        disorienting
just as everyone's undone:
                rivers wither into the sea.

Polygonum fagopyrum

In the Dry Garden

gray mouse springs
over the sidewalk—
weeds dance

summer buckwheat
pink thimble flowers—
fall honey

marigolds bent west
              desert wind
sharp orange blooms
              scatter

comfrey's long green leaves
purple bells
   beside the boulevard's
        din and growl

small white butterfly
blown off its flower—
motorcycle full throttle

tall dry stems
          bursting blue gray pods
sage
     strewn

lavender flowers
        litter the dirt—
bees, butterflies

by the firehouse wall
arugula, comfrey, tomato vines—
greens ablaze

summer squash, peach tree
five story fan palm—
drought

garden chair splintering—
soon to plant
    the hapless planter

Symphytum officinale

THE NAP

In the afternoon, wanting takes a nap
   even busy people occasionally sleep

  squirrels survey their city of trees
  crow appetites slumber
  we rest our heads.

When shadows more steeply slant
      we wake.
Where were we when this freshet of dreams
       transported us far away?

We resort to our memory of needs
    and carry on.

WILD PLUM BLOSSOMS

rounding black ragged trunks
clouds of spring breath
      exhaled into winter air

CALIFORNIA FAN PALM

cracked concrete
       small green wing unfolds
freeway off ramp

Sycamores in Sullivan Canyon

dun leaves fall
      crisp heaps
dry stream

Platanus occidentalis

NEW ROOMMATE

headache
heat and labor
delighted heart—

daughter moves in

Any Time of Day

Cat laps from the
bathtub faucet.
Colorado River
drip
drip
drip

LULLABY

All night crickets see-saw sing
                beneath my
kitchen window.
Sleeping camellias.

FACING THE MIRROR

The skin of the fruit
I once peeled
peels me.

Patchwork hair
thick, thin, sparse
coaxed to curls—
gels and sprays.

Iris tenax

Liquid tan
patted and smoothed—
a dusting of powder
a veiling of years.

Feathered short hairs
over each eye
dyed or penciled—
Arcs de Triomphe.

Velour or pink spice
lipstick smoothed over
pale lips.

Crepis barbata

Lupinus sabinianus

THE SALON

Women at the nail salon
        middle aged and younger
lips puffed
        extra-large and hardened
            no soft pillows for smooching
the smacked-in-the mouth look
        not prize fighters—
                warrior lips
red walls
        whitened teeth
                endless war.

ASH

gray silk
mutes the red maples—
nearby hills
inferno

mayfly swarm
swirling
coats the windshield

fire spun
diaphanous
shrouds my lungs

Nemophila insignis

The Dishes

Duty dishes rattle
     rhythmic with the washer's bones
silencing sorrows
         gray motes
     like mice that can't be trapped
shuttling beneath the cabinets.

I Have to Warn You

Trash bag in tatters
    black moths
        blowing around the garden
plastic cups cans clotted dust wadded Kleenex
    heaped
        on the backyard path
the garden plot gone to thistle
on the trellis berry vines brown.

Take my word for it
    meet me out front.

SOUTH ON THE 5

San Joaquin Valley fog trapped among branches
                    identically hewn
                            any stray reach, exuberant, light hungry
              cut to shape for easy mechanical harvest
Fruiting food slaves, force fed
                    unable to not blossom and bear
                                not die until uprooted—
                        better profits elsewhere

KITCHEN WINDOW

Hot pink zinnias and Gerber daisy petals
    dyed or bred hard for high color
    shed themselves like commas on a blue table.
Honeysuckle scrambles along the side yard fence
        thick old branches molded to the boards
    ignores the pretty flowers
    drooped in their vase.
Zinnias mark the vine a prisoner
    tied to a cross
    denied water at the crucial moment.
Meanwhile the pinks wilt and die
    in their pretty cup.

Hunger

The shock of slaughter wears off—
aroma from enticing flesh
    lifts the fork
    to the mouth.

Eschscholzia californica

Hope and Love

i

The belly of hope
                    like nope
        has a hole in it.

Wonder
        like one
                    ever-brims
        with all that is.

ii

Love's O
            rests
                        in the lap of L
    safe from the vice
                    of the following V
    ends with E
                    as in we
    winged from the perch of love
    like song sparrows.

PANDEMIC

In the morning two crows
   rummage wrappers
         blown into the gutter

A gray man sits on the curb
   slumped beside
         strewn burdens

The old maple
   trunk bent between sidewalk and street
      spring branches
         errant with buds

Last night I rent memory for words
      these wrappers
      still empty.

THIS TIME THIS PLACE
—after Tu Fu

I lie alone in my queen size bed
    covered by pale flannel
        worn thin by decades of wash
The refrigerator in the next room
      clanks on
           noisy motor drones
                through the wall
Sirens whirl red red   red red
                against the window shade
Street lights glare, signs,
        headlamps, illuminated windows
            overwhelm even the moon
Abandoned shadows flee upward, loosed
          toward infinity.

Behind my sleep mask
I feel my way deeper into darkness and wait.

SUSAN SUNTREE is an award-winning poet, essayist, and community activist. Her work is published in journals and anthologies, and includes essays and book chapters about feminist and environmental theatre. Books of poetry include *Dear Traveler* (Finishing Line Press) and the non-fiction epic poem *Sacred Sites: The Secret History of Southern California* (University of Nebraska Press), written with the guidance of award-winning Western scientists and indigenous Southern California Culture Bearers, and released in a recently updated paperback edition and audiobook. A *Los Angeles Times* bestseller, awards include the Southern California Independent Booksellers Association Award for Nonfiction, PEN Oakland Josephine Miles Award for Narrative Poetry, the Mellon Foundation's Elemental Arts Award; the audiobook was a finalist for a Society of Voice Arts and Sciences prize. Other books include *Eye of the Womb* (Power Press, poetry), also published in Madrid as a bilingual edition, *El Ojo de la Matriz* (Vision Libros); *Tulips* (Exiled-in-America Press, poetry), a bilingual chapbook of translations of poetry by Spanish poet Ana Rossetti; *Rita Moreno* (Chelsea Press) YA biography; *Wisdom of the East; Stories of Compassion, Inspiration and Love* (Contemporary Books) with a foreword by His Holiness the Dalai Lama.

www.susansuntree.com